Illustrated Tacky Trivia

Rick Detorie

A Perigee Book

Perigee Books
are published by
The Putnam Publishing Group
200 Madison Avenue
New York, NY 10016

Copyright © 1985 by Rick Detorie
All rights reserved. This book, or parts thereof,
may not be reproduced in any form without permission.
Published simultaneously in Canada by
General Publishing Co. Limited, Toronto

Library of Congress Cataloging-in-Publication Data

Detorie, Rick.
Illustrated tacky trivia.

"A Perigee book."
1. Questions and answers.   2. American wit
and humor.   I. Title.
AG195.D47   1985   031'.02   85-12418
ISBN 0-399-51182-2

Printed in the United States of America
1 2 3 4 5 6 7 8 9 10

To Channing Clarkson, the most famous person I know.

Special thanks to Sandy Detorie for her invaluable (because she wasn't paid) research.

1 What U.S. city has the highest murder rate?

2 What African dictator said, "I eat them before they eat me"?

3 What bathroom fixtures did Joan Crawford change every time she changed husbands?

4 What social disease is nicknamed the "curse of Venus"?

5 What Italian leader had a mortal fear of cripples, open umbrellas, and hunchbacks?

6 What are the two most popular methods by which teenage boys kill themselves?

7 According to a recent poll, what part of their body did most Americans like least?

8 What does the average person release one and a half quarts of per day?

9 What female rock star, popular in the '60s, had been nominated in college for the title "Ugliest Man on Campus"?

10 What actress starred in the sexploitation film *The Stud*?

11 What hard rocker bit the head off a bat onstage at a Des Moines concert?

12 On whose tombstone is written, "On the whole, I'd rather be in Philadelphia"?

13 What is the most common cause of choking in America?

14 Name one of three professional golfers struck by lightning during the same tournament in June 1975.

15 What is the middle name of Cathy Smith, the woman accused of fatally injecting John Belushi with speedballs?

16 On what kids' show from the '50s did a confused little boy urinate into a jack-o'-lantern while on the air?

17 What U.S. president hated cats so much that he ordered any found on the grounds of his home to be shot?

18 In what state is the town of Intercourse?

19 What British punk rock group had as members Captain Sensible, Dave Vanian, and Rat Scabies?

20 In Spain, the weapon mace is called "mate suegra." What does "mate suegra" mean literally?

21 Of Napoleon, Julius Caesar, and Josef Stalin, which leader suffered from epilepsy?

22 Who once told Frank Sinatra, "Make yourself at home, Frank. Hit somebody"?

23 What European country has been ruled at various times by Charles the Fat, Louis the Stammerer, and Charles the Simple?

24 In the game of poker, what is the dead man's hand?

25 What kind of woman is it bad luck for a baseball player to spot in the stands?

26 What was the name of the man who inadvertently filmed John F. Kennedy's assassination?

27 What is the most common contagious illness?

28 In what TV miniseries did actress Phoebe Cates confront three women with, "All right, which one of you bitches is my mother?"

29 For what crime was Bruno Richard Hauptmann executed?

30 According to superstition, if a woman puts her husband's hand in a pail of water while he's asleep, what will he do?

31 Of Whom is Saint Marculf the patron saint?

32 Who said,, "There are three things my brother Chico is always on: a phone, a horse, or a broad"?

33 What is it against the law for animals to do in public in Stanfield, Oregon?

34 What '60s rock star took too many sleeping pills and died of suffocation, having inhaled his own vomit?

35 What prescription drug is nicknamed "dillies," "footballs," and "big D"?

36 How many witches did Dorothy kill in *The Wizard of Oz?*

37 How many of his six wives did Henry VIII have beheaded?

38 What racy novel has as its subtitle *Memoirs of a Woman of Pleasure?*

39 What social philosopher and author of *Das Kapital* seldom bathed and for the last twenty years of his life was afflicted with boils all over his body?

40 On which day of the week do more men die suddenly from heart attacks?

41 What famous Hollywood character actor was buried in a vampire costume?

42 What part of Sarah Bernhardt's anatomy did P. T. Barnum once offer to buy?

43 What was the name of the chairman of the House Ways and Means Committee who was involved in a sex scandal with stripper Fanne Foxe in 1974?

44 About what was John De Lorean speaking when he said, "This stuff's as good as gold"?

45 What kind of creature is the black-eared bushtit?

46 What writer did Truman Capote describe as a "truck driver in drag"?

47 What part of her body did comedienne Totie Fields lose shortly before her death?

48 What rock star did the Hell's Angels vow to kill after Altamont?

49 As a child, what Russian ruler tortured animals and threw dogs from rooftops?

50 What U.S. airport is considered by the IFALPA as the most dangerous in the world?

51 What was the name of the 1972 film in which transvestite "Divine" eats dog excrement?

52 What European princess gave birth a mere six months after her wedding in December 1983?

53 Besides sex, to what daily ritual did Mae West attribute her longevity and youthful appearance?

54 What was the name of Patty Hearst's roommate at the time of their arrest in 1975?

55 How did the ancient Celts execute their criminals?

56 What female rock star appeared in the 1979 sexploitation film *A Certain Sacrifice?*

57 What common domestic creature did people in the Middle Ages fear as an incarnation of the devil?

58 What do Elizabeth Taylor and Jacqueline Onassis both wear in a size ten?

59 What put Karen Ann Quinlan into a coma?

60 In what state did the plane carrying Buddy Holly crash?

61 Where is the country of Nauru, which relies on the export of bird droppings as its main source of income?

62 Besides "Baby," what other pet name did Gertrude Stein use to address her lover, Alice B. Toklas?

63 Who called Geraldine Ferraro a "four-million-dollar . . . I can't say it, but it rhymes with rich"?

64 Of spitting, farting, and belching, what do the Masai tribesmen of Tanzania and Kenya do as a greeting?

65 What husband and wife singing duo, popular in the '60s and '70s, didn't actually marry each other until 1969, just prior to their daughter's birth?

66 The Greek poet Aeschylus was killed when an eagle mistook his bald head for a rock and dropped what on him?

67 What religion does Michael Jackson hustle door-to-door?

68 What is the prime ingredient of Mexican mole sauce?

69 What tacky breed of dog is the most popular in the U.S.?

70 What dashing Hollywood leading man, who died a chronic alcoholic, also had tuberculosis, sinusitis, emphysema, a heart murmur, chronic irritation of the urethra, and gonorrhea at the time of his death?

71 What World War II general ordered his men, "Do not needlessly endanger your lives until I give you the signal"?

72 In what country was Paul McCartney jailed for carrying a half pound of marijuana?

73 What big-city mayor warned that he was going to be so tough that he would "make Attila the Hun look like a faggot"?

74 Among mammals, which one has the highest number of sperm per ejaculation?

75 What happened on *The Dick Cavett Show* soon after guest J. I. Rodale said he was so healthy that he planned to live for a long time?

76 What is the title given to the head of the Ku Klux Klan?

77 What male rock star was once elected Homecoming Queen by the University of Houston?

78 Of lethal gas, electrocution, and lethal injection, which method of execution is the most widely used in the U.S.?

79 Which member of the British Royal Family referred to Boy George as a "tart"?

80 What Hollywood actor served two months in jail in 1948 for possession of marijuana?

81 To what magazine did Jimmy Carter admit that he committed adultery in his heart many times?

82 What did Madame Curie, the discoverer of radium, die from?

83 Why did Dorothy Parker name her pet parrot Onan?

84 About which pitcher did Earl Weaver say, "Every single gray hair I got, I got from [him]"?

85 In Korea, what is the main ingredient of the soup *baim tang*?

86 What Hollywood star, when told by a man that he was six feet seven inches, replied, "Let's forget about the six feet and talk about the seven inches"?

87 What does *mushin,* a term for an altered state of consciousness in Zen training, mean?

88 What entertainer was known in his early years as "Silent Sam, the Dancing Midget"?

89 What was the name of Mike Curb's singing group, about whom Tricia Nixon once said, "If I have to hear them one more time, I'll vomit"?

90 What U.S. state has the highest alcohol consumption?

91 Brussels's best-known statue is the twenty-inch figure of a boy called the "Manneken-Pis." What is the boy doing?

92 What type of criminal in the U.S. is most likely to sport a tattoo?

93 What rock group destroyed a dressing room and stage when their promoter failed to remove the brown M & M's from the two pounds of candy they had ordered?

94 What TV character was the first to openly experience menopause?

95 How many dead chinchillas does it take to make an average chinchilla coat?

96 What professional baseball player was slapped with a paternity suit in 1922 by a teenage girl claiming statutory rape?

97 According to the London *Sunday Times,* what physical attribute do most women admire about men?

98 From what aging Hollywood star did Angie Dickinson allegedly "steal" Burt Bacharach?

99 Three of the Horsemen of the Apocalypse were Conquest, Famine, and Pestilence. Who was the fourth?

100 At what age does the average person begin to lose about 100,000 brain cells a day?

101 What president told Gene Autry to give his regards to his wife Dale?

102 In what city was Olympic medalist Edwin Moses arrested in 1984 for soliciting a prostitute?

103 According to the legend, what was the total number of whacks that Lizzie Borden gave her parents?

104 What was the name of the child actress in the sitcom *Family Affair* who died of a drug overdose at eighteen?

105 What early rock and roll star spent two years in federal prison for violating the Mann Act?

106 From what team was professional baseball relief pitcher Steve Howe cut for using cocaine?

107 What Russian leader said, "A single death is a tragedy, a million deaths is a statistic"?

108 What member of the Sex Pistols stabbed his girlfriend to death, then committed suicide?

109 What is a castrated rooster called?

110 Into what part of his victims' bodies was gangster Israel "Icepick" Alderman especially skilled at pressing an icepick?

111 Why was Korean evangelist Sun Myung Moon sentenced to eighteen months in a federal prison?

112 From what university was Senator Edward Kennedy suspended for cheating in 1951?

113 According to superstition, what happens to a person who sneezes four times in a row?

114 What European leader said, "Anyone who sees and paints a sky green and pastures blue ought to be sterilized"?

115 In medieval castles, what was the garderobe?

116 What legendary actress of backbone and bite said, "All I want . . . is a decent script, a competent cast, and a good director. The rest is a crock of shit"?

117 What was the name of the professional skier who was shot and killed by Claudine Longet?

118 In what city was the Coconut Grove nightclub, where a fire in 1942 killed 491 people?

119 What '60s black radical said that violence is as American as cherry pie?

120 Where did Skylab crash?

121 What is the preferred method of suicide in the United States?

122 What is the most dangerous breed of dog?

123 Of Leonardo da Vinci, Michelangelo, and Donatello, which one was born illegitimate?

124 What *Saturday Night Live* colleague did Laraine Newman describe as "an incredible slob. He wore shorts, wouldn't bathe for days . . . and [went] around with six days' growth on his face"?

125 In what U.S. state is death by firing squad the preferred method of execution?

126 Which of Conrad Hilton's wives said, "Conrad and I had one thing in common. We both wanted his money"?

127 In California, what is the only animal that it's not illegal to shoot at from a car?

128 Where is the Fresh Kills Landfill, the world's biggest garbage dump?

129 What was the nickname of the atomic bomb dropped on Nagasaki, Japan, in 1945?

130 What was the name of the 1969 Beatles' album which spurred rumors of Paul McCartney's death?

131 What did one woman claim in a successful lawsuit that a San Francisco cable car accident had caused her to become?

132 What ancient Jewish queen was chopped up and fed to stray dogs so that her remains would be spread about the town as dog do?

133 According to the nursery rhyme, where did Peter, Peter, Pumpkin-eater, put his wife?

134 What was the name of the church founded by Maharaj Ji, the pudgy teen-aged guru?

135 In what low-budget 1964 film did Pia Zadora appear as an elf?

136 How was accused spy Mata Hari executed?

137 In what year was D. H. Lawrence's *Lady Chatterley's Lover* finally published unexpurgated in the U.S.?

138 How were the Salem witches put to death?

139 Which of the principal stars of *Gone With the Wind* wore false teeth?

140 In 1982, a twenty-seven-year-old man was killed when he fired two shotgun blasts at a large plant, causing it to fall and crush him. What kind of plant was the killer?

141 In what part of the body is the Houston's muscle?

142 The host of what TV talk show discovered that "psychic" Uri Geller was using magic tricks?

143 What feminist said, "A woman reading *Playboy* feels a little like a Jew reading a Nazi manual"?

144 What did Edward R. Murrow, Nat King Cole, and John Wayne all die of?

145 On which continent did rats originate?

146 How many victims were involved between 1979 and 1981 in the "Atlanta Child Murders"?

147 What state outlawed a 1959 children's book, *The Rabbits' Wedding*, because a white rabbit married a black one?

148 Whose rear end did Napoleon Bonaparte once describe as "the prettiest little backside imaginable"?

149 Sex-film star Marilyn Chambers appeared as a model on the box of what brand of laundry detergent?

150 What did Thomas Crapper invent?

151 What macho American writer committed suicide by firing a gun into his mouth?

152 What did Leo Durocher refuse to change all through the Giants' 1951 pennant drive?

153 Actress Elsa Lanchester *(The Bride of Frankenstein)* was struck deaf for a week when her husband, Charles Laughton, confessed what to her?

154 What U.S. city has the most abortions and the most lawyers?

155 What president said, "The Italians . . . you can't find one who is honest"?

156 What has a person who has immolated himself done?

29

157 Why didn't the dogs who played Lassie on the TV series ever get pregnant?

158 What is the only X-rated movie to win the Academy Award as best picture?

159 What position of influence and power did the father of murderers Cesare and Lucrezia Borgia hold?

160 What does a person with polydactylism have more than the usual number of?

161 After the first game of the 1980 World Series, the Royals' star hitter, George Brett, was hospitalized. What was his ailment?

162 Name one of the two U.S. presidents who carried bullets in their bodies.

163 The fattest dog on record weighed 295 lbs. What breed was it?

164 What teenage sitcom costar was fired from her show because she was unable to function normally because of cocaine abuse?

165 What convicted murderer and cult leader proclaimed that "Hitler had the best answers to everything"?

166 What play was showing at Ford's Theater the night Lincoln was assassinated?

167 The IRS's "Dinah Shore Ruling" allows actresses to write off their gowns as a business deduction on one condition. What is that condition?

168 Who was aboard the yacht *Splendour* the night Natalie Wood drowned?

169 What part of a chameleon is as long as its body?

170 What killed silent-screen star Rudolph Valentino?

171 What European country banned Donald Duck cartoons on grounds of immorality because he wasn't married to Daisy Duck?

172 What imposing-looking country singer starred in the 1967 film *Door-to-Door Maniac,* in which he sang "I've Come to Kill" and "Five Minutes to Live"?

173 After firearms, what is the most popular method of murder in the U.S.?

174 What Egyptian queen married two of her brothers and afterward had them put to death?

175 What disease is known as the "kissing disease"?

176 What president's mother said: "Sometimes when I look at all my children, I say to myself, you should have remained a virgin"?

177 In what federal prison were Julius and Ethel Rosenberg executed?

178 What breed of dog did Grace Kelly sleep with for most of her adult life?

179 What national championship contest is held every April in Beaver, Oklahoma?

180 How did Art Linkletter's daughter, Diane, kill herself?

181 What do anthropophagites eat?

182 Besides caffeine, what other stimulant was included in the original formula for Coca-Cola?

183 What U.S. president's corpse has been moved seventeen times since his death and in 1876 was stolen by grave robbers?

184 Early in his career, what *Bonanza* star had his large, protruding ears surgically pulled back?

185 To what wealthy Greek did Eva Perón make love for one night and cook an omelet, for which he paid her $10,000?

186 What did Marilyn Monroe bleach because she "wanted to feel blond all over"?

187 According to rumor, where were F. Scott Fitzgerald and Sheila Graham when he suffered his fatal heart attack?

188 What country has the highest murder rate?

189 What was the name of the convict who spent a record of eleven years and ten months on death row in San Quentin Prison before being executed May 2, 1960?

190 What San Francisco–based punk rock band had albums entitled *Fresh Fruit for Rotting Vegetables* and *Plastic Surgery Disasters*?

191 What *Dallas* star claims that she got where she is by being "a black widow spider. Screw 'em and eat 'em"?

192 Whom did Arthur Bremer try to assassinate?

193 Which of his ears did van Gogh cut off?

194 According to the Madame Tussaud's Wax Museum 1981 Annual Poll, who is the most hated person in history?

195 In what country was the Jonestown mass suicide-murder?

196 What U.S. state has the highest per capita rate of venereal disease?

197 In the 1964 movie *Goldfinger,* what was the name of Goldfinger's lesbian accomplice who ran a flying school for women?

198 How many youths did Bernhard Goetz shoot on the New York City subway in December 1984?

199 What comedian said, "I knew Doris Day before she was a virgin"?

200 Where did Queen Victoria hang a picture of her dead husband Albert's corpse?

201 In what ancient country were red-haired men sacrificed to the god Osiris?

202 What female rock star named her daughter "god," but later changed it to "China"?

203 What was the name of the flu that swept the U.S. in 1957 and 1958, killing 60,000?

204 What *Today Show* host killed himself with a shotgun blast in 1982?

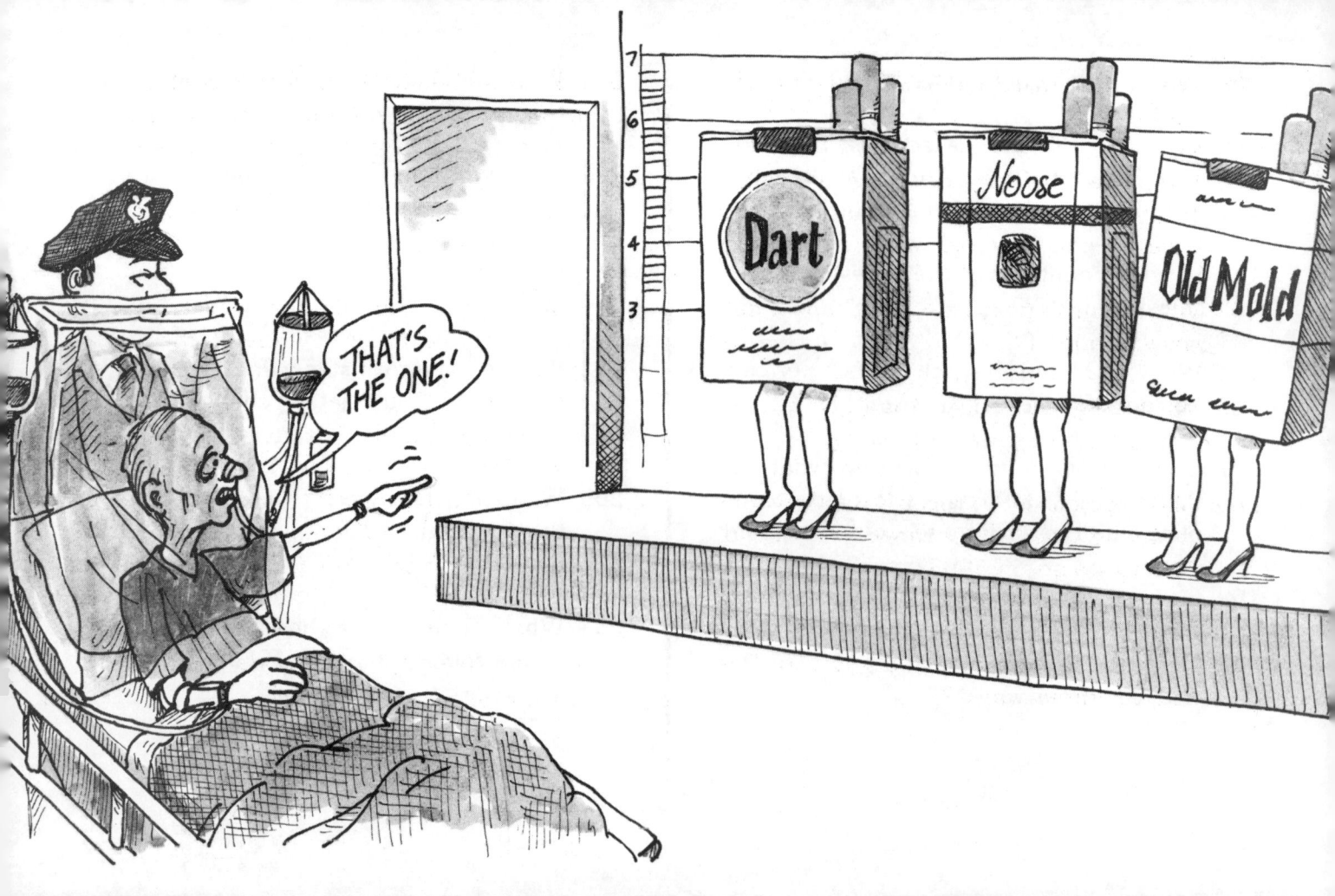

205 What is the most popular cigarette in the world?

206 Jerry Lee Lewis's career came to a halt in 1957 when he married his cousin, Myra Gale Brown. How old was the bride?

207 What is bird's nest soup, the Chinese delicacy, made of?

208 What drugs did Edgar Allan Poe rely on to relieve his severe depressions?

209 What reason did Françoise Gilot give for divorcing her 82-year-old husband, Pablo Picasso, in 1963?

210 What American president told reporters, "I'm never through with a girl until I've had her three ways"?

211 What well-known nineteenth-century author of children's stories photographed naked prepubescent girls as a hobby?

212 On approximately 85% of all men, which testicle hangs lower?

213 What color hair did Judas Iscariot and most of the other villains of the Bible have?

214 What was the title of Sylvester Stallone's porn film *A Party at Kitty and Stud's* later changed to?

215 What successful off-Broadway musical featured the song "Sodomy"?

216 What singer appeared nude on her *Hard Times for Lovers* album?

217 Through most of the Middle Ages, decapitation was reserved for the aristocracy. How were members of the lower classes executed?

218 What blind singer was the spokesman for Pioneer's Laserdisc Video Player?

219 What major U.S. city has the highest auto theft rate?

220 According to ancient Greek superstition, what physical characteristics did the wild hyena change every year?

221 On his statue of what biblical character did Michelangelo put horns?

222 What flamboyant, gravel-voiced actress said, "Cocaine isn't habit forming. I should know—I've been using it for years"?

223 Napoleon's chief surgeon holds the record of thirteen to fifteen seconds for performing what kind of surgery?

224 At what airport were Tony Perkins, Stacy Keach, and Linda McCartney all arrested at different times on drug-related charges?

225 What was Henry VIII's wife, Anne Boleyn, said to have had three of?

226 Which state has the most potholes?

227 Which of the Beach Boys let Charles Manson stay at his house about a year before the Sharon Tate murders?

228 What powerful and influential person (besides Sam Giancana) did Judith Exner claim to have known intimately?

41

229 What kind of animal was used to test the first parachute?

230 About whom did H. R. Haldeman say, "He was the weirdest man ever to live in the White House"?

231 Of syphilis, high blood pressure, and leprosy, which disease is most prevalent in the U.S. today?

232 What president caught pneumonia during his inauguration and died one month into his term?

233 Who did the *People* magazine poll overwhelmingly name as 1980's most boring man on TV?

234 What personal possession of Charlie Chaplin's was held for $600,000 ransom in 1978?

235 What state has the most murders per capita?

236 In what year did Eddie Fisher declare bankruptcy?

237 What American tycoon claimed to have slept with Carole Lombard, Marilyn Monroe, and Jean Peters?

238 In 1971, when John Rosenberg founded est, what did he change his name to?

239 From what Nevada resort was Frank Sinatra, Jr., kidnapped?

240 Who did onetime manicurist Sandra Bernhard describe as the worst tipper in the universe?

241 Who was the only U.S. president to perform in Las Vegas?

242 What was the name of the only American serviceman shot for desertion (1944)?

243 Who did the Charles Manson "family" murder the night after the Sharon Tate murders?

244 During the 1984 presidential campaign, Gary Hart said he was born in 1937. In what year was he actually born?

245 According to the nursery rhyme, who put Pussy in the well?

246 What comic admitted that he wrote his autobiography "more to be able to mention that Jack Kennedy and I were friends than anything else"?

247 In Kentucky, what is it illegal for a married man to purchase unless he's accompanied by his wife?

248 What did pop singer Fabian do in 1974 that he later regretted because he looked "fat and stupid"?

249 Which is more popular in the U.S., murder or suicide?

250 What Hollywood cowboy told his wife: "When I go, just skin me and put me on top of Trigger"?

251 What rock star's biography was entitled *No One Here Gets Out Alive?*

252 What is the biggest killer of teenagers in the U.S.?

45

253 What political activist and Oscar-winning actress suffered from bulimia in her teens and early twenties?

254 In what country was suttee (the custom of burning a dead man's living widow along with his remains) practiced?

255 What newsman did Ronald Reagan refer to as "the Ayatollah of the White House press corps"?

256 Who was the fattest U.S. president?

257 What is the most common respiratory ailment among school-age children?

258 What U.S. state has had the highest known cases of leprosy?

259 Which of Albert Einstein's organs was not buried with the rest of his body?

260 What job prior to her modeling career did Lauren Hutton find humiliating because "patrons assumed you were a whore"?

261 What breed of dog was Pushinka, the dog presented to President Kennedy by Khrushchev in 1961?

262 According to the medieval English *Boke of Curtasye*, it was proper etiquette to blow one's nose with a finger as long as it was later wiped where?

263 What did Faye Emerson and Jayne Mansfield both accidentally reveal on live television?

264 In the world of professional horse racing, when is a horse a "maiden"?

265 What was the name of the woman who "won" the Boston marathon after taking a subway to the finish line?

266 What actress did Joan Rivers say had more chins than a Chinese phone book?

267 What U.S. president recommended, "Get plenty of atomic bombs on hand, drop one on Stalin, put the U.N. to work, and set up a free world"?

268 What animal is used more than any other in U.S. laboratory experiments?

269 Which member of the Beach Boys lived for years as a recluse in his Bel Air mansion, which was equipped with a recording studio and a sandbox?

270 What did Russian Czar Peter the Great once personally cut off each of his noblemen?

271 Why did an Arab sheik offer Joan Collins's first husband $10,000?

272 What Chinese leader once dropped his pants in front of foreign dignitaries because he needed to "cool off"?

273 With whom did the Beatles claim they continued to communicate after his death in 1967?

274 In what part of the United States is the divorce rate highest?

275 Where did the one survivor hide during Richard Speck's torture and murder spree which left eight student nurses dead in 1966?

276 What pianist has his own museum in Las Vegas?

277 What was Lady Godiva protesting by riding nude on horseback?

278 During the mating season, male mandrill baboons often display their genitals. What three colors make up that area?

279 Tennis player and doctor Richard Raskind underwent a sex-change operation. Who did Raskind become?

280 What part of Napoleon's anatomy was removed after his death and later offered for auction?

281 Which star of TV's *Starsky and Hutch* was arrested in 1982 for wife-beating?

282 On what day of the week do the fewest men die of heart attacks?

283 What was the name of the soft-core porn star with whom England's Prince Andrew had a brief but well-publicized dalliance?

284 What famous stripper wrote *The G-String Murders?*

285 To what part of the body might one find a buildup of cerumen?

286 About what was S. I. Hayakawa speaking when he said that we should keep it because we stole it fair and square?

287 What U.S. president stopped having marital relations with his wife in 1917?

288 What did Larry Flynt use to fashion the diaper he wore into a court of law in 1984?

289 Are elderly people more likely to die in the months preceding their birthdays, or the months that follow?

290 What country had the highest percentage of its people killed during World War II?

291 In the Middle Ages, what was the name given to pies made from animal kidneys, hearts, livers, and entrails?

292 What U.S. city ranks first in per capita consumption of alcohol?

293 Why was Deborah Ann Fountain, Miss New York, disqualified from the 1981 Miss U.S.A. Pageant?

294 About whom did the 1983 *Us* magazine readers' poll say, "She doesn't buy her clothes in the five and dime; she just looks that way"?

295 In what horror movie did Steve McQueen rescue a town from a large, squirming slab of flab?

296 What did astronomer Galileo study so intently through his telescope that it eventually caused him to go blind?

297 In what Texas city did sniper Charles Whitman shoot fifteen people from a tower in 1966?

298 About which of his costars did Tony Curtis say, "Kissing her was like kissing Hitler"?

299 What did Joan Crawford refuse to allow done to her while she was having her period?

300 Who was the "Son of Sam" killer?

301 What are "Tarita" and "Tehotu" to Marlon Brando?

302 How many students were killed by National Guardsmen at Kent State University in 1970?

303 What singer, according to a member of her rock group, died not from choking, but of a heart attack brought on by heroin?

304 In 1924 a convicted criminal named Lee Jon was the first person to be executed in this manner. How did he die?

305 What do 80% of fat children grow up to be?

306 What famous tenor was tried in 1906 in the "Monkey House Scandal"?

307 What porn-film star, after becoming a born-again Christian, claimed that she had been drugged and forced to perform before the cameras?

308 What U.S. president was so fearful of being trapped in a fire that he practiced crawling around the floors of the White House?

309 What part of her anatomy did Hitler's mistress, Eva Braun, have surgically enlarged?

310 According to the FBI, during what season do most burglaries occur?

311 What blonde TV policewoman said, "I dress for women and I undress for men"?

312 On average, how many unidentified bodies turn up each day in the United States?

313 What eighteenth-century monarch was rumored to have been killed while trying to make love to a horse?

314 What part of the camel do desert Arabs use as medicine and hair tonic?

315 Within five minutes, how often does someone in the United States commit suicide?

316 Who declared that he was the first man "to piss his pants on the moon"?

317 Who won the Nobel Peace Prize in 1972?

318 Who wrote the bawdy "1601: Conversation, as It Was at the Social Fireside in the Time of the Tudors"?

319 What was the name given to Rosemary's baby?

320 Early French kings stuck three hairs in the seal of official documents. From where did they pluck the hairs?

321 In the back seat of what kind of car did Hank Williams die?

322 To whom did Lyndon Johnson say in public, "When I want your advice, I'll give it to you"?

323 Most Australian aborigines are not ashamed of their nakedness or of defecating in front of others. What are they embarrassed to be seen doing?

324 What did Moses recommend for victims of gonorrhea?

325 In ancient times, before champagne, what was splattered against a new ship for good luck?

326 What book was Mark David Chapman carrying when he shot John Lennon?

327 Is alcohol consumption heavier in the northern states or the South?

328 What is the name of Al Goldstein's sex-oriented tabloid?

329 What '70s R & B singer switched to gospel singing after his girlfriend poured boiling grits on him, then killed herself with his gun?

330 Of the British Museum, the Kinsey Institute, and the Vatican Library, which has the largest collection of books on sex?

331 How much was Spiro Agnew fined for income tax evasion?

332 During the Middle Ages, what "crime" could you have been accused of if your pet disobeyed, you floated on water, or you had a mole on your body?

333 In ancient Israel the zarah was a "tight woman." What was the zonah?

334 What Hollywood leading man of the silent era was arrested in 1916 in a vice and white slavery investigation?

335 On which side did Adolf Hitler part his hair?

336 What group's lead singer said: "I am not a snob. Ask anybody. Well, anybody who matters"?

337 According to the ABC News–Harris Survey, what is the favorite leisure activity of most Americans?

338 What presidential relative did *Esquire* magazine name "Primate of the Decade" in 1980?

339 What was the first musical instrument that Barry Manilow played?

340 What does a hepatologist specialize in treating?

341 With what famous actor did Shelley Winters fool around every Christmas for many years?

342 What German church leader branded Pope Leo X "no better than any other stinking sinner"?

343 How did George Reeves, TV's Superman, die?

344 What 1968 presidential candidate said, "If any demonstrator ever lays down in front of my car, it'll be the last car he'll ever lay down in front of"?

345 Movie mogul Adolph Zukor claimed that he lived to be 100 because of something he did at 98. What was it?

346 What room of the house was Archie Bunker's library?

347 What movie comedian said, "I am free of all prejudices. I hate everyone equally"?

348 In the novel *Moby Dick*, what is Captain Ahab's artificial leg made of?

349 In the 1954 movie *Them*, what vegetable did James Arness play?

350 What brand of beer did Gary Gilmore request on the morning of his execution?

351 How many American teenagers have sexual intercourse for the first time each day?

352 Who had a comedy album entitled *That Nigger Is Crazy?*

353 What British rock singer was once a gravedigger in London?

354 In the novel *Valley of the Dolls*, what did Jennifer North do rather than go through with a mastectomy?

355 How many days were the U.S. hostages held in Iran?

356 What happened to Connie Francis in 1974 that caused her to seek psychiatric treatment for two and a half years?

357 Before deciding on the bald eagle, what bird did Ben Franklin originally want established as America's national symbol?

358 What did Mahatma Gandhi receive every night at bedtime?

359 On what charges was boxing promoter Don King indicted on twenty-three counts in 1984?

360 Actress Clara Bow reputedly made love to the entire football team of what U.S. college?

361 Eating a mouse was an ancient remedy for what common ailment?

362 What commercial was Michael Jackson shooting when his hair caught fire?

363 What Roman god protected a husband's sperm?

364 For how much was the palimony suit brought against the Alfred Bloomingdale estate by his mistress Vicki Morgan?

365 What presidential election ticket did wags nickname "Fritz and Tits"?

366 What do boxers do into their gloves for luck before a bout?

367 What rock star lamented that she had ridden on a train with 365 men on board, but she'd had sex with only 65 of them?

368 Alfred Packer is the only man in the U.S. to have been convicted of what crime?

369 Where was Martin Luther King, Jr., when he was gunned down?

370 From what South American country did the killer bees escape?

371 About what beat-generation writer did Truman Capote say, "That's not writing, that's typing"?

372 Late in his life and because of his tremendous fear of germs, what did Howard Hughes use when touching anything?

373 Where did the ancient Tauri people display the severed heads of their enemies?

374 What was Albert DeSalvo also known as?

375 With the exception of the Apollo 11 astronauts in 1969, what do all the people depicted on U.S. postage stamps have in common?

376 Who replaced Vanessa Williams as Miss America after the *Penthouse* magazine scandal?

377 What did Karen Carpenter die of?

378 What member of Crosby, Still, Nash, and Young was sentenced to five years in jail for cocaine possession and carrying a loaded weapon?

379 What Swedish film director said, "Everything is worth precisely as much as a belch, the difference being that a belch is more satisfying"?

380 How long does it take the average human being to completely shed the outer layer of skin?

381 On which arm did Captain Hook sport his hook?

382 Who played murderer Perry Smith in the film version of *In Cold Blood?*

383 What star of TV's *Lassie* was arrested on drug-related charges in 1972, 1975, and 1980?

384 What country has the highest suicide rate?

385 Where were the famous twins, Chang and Eng, joined?

386 What is the name of the man who shot and killed Marvin Gaye?

387 What is the most prevalent infectious disease in the world?

388 What part of his anatomy did J. Paul Getty III lose during his kidnapping ordeal?

389 Where on his face was Mao Tse-tung's wart?

390 What former member of the Rolling Stones was found dead in his swimming pool, the coroner's report citing "death by misadventure"?

391 What's the official method of execution in Japan?

392 What unusual collection did J. Edgar Hoover keep locked in a drawer of his desk?

393 What popular '50s quizmaster said, "A man is only as old as the woman he feels"?

394 What James Taylor song chronicled his stay in a mental institution?

395 What *Rebel Without a Cause* costar was stabbed to death in Los Angeles in 1975?

396 What unusual collection of lifelike objects does Michael Jackson keep in a room of his house?

397 By what U.S. president did slave Sally Hayes have five children?

398 For what Italian director did Ingrid Bergman leave her husband "to live in sin" in 1949?

399 What *Bonanza* star played the werewolf in the film *I Was a Teenage Werewolf*?

400 What German religious leader was so anti-Semitic that he recommended burning the synagogues, confiscating Jewish books, and deporting all Jews to Palestine?

401 What is a person who sniffs armpits (for deodorant effectiveness) for a living called?

402 What did Elvis Presley call his penis?

403 What successful inventor worked in a rat-infested lab, wore smelly clothes, and starved himself because he thought food was poison?

404 After her Miss America win in 1982, it was uncovered that Debra Sue Maffett had had cosmetic surgery. What part of her body had been rearranged?

405 What disease did Jenny die of in *Love Story*?

406 The game of soccer is believed to have started in ancient times by a group of Roman soldiers. What did they use as a ball?

407 From what city did Jimmy Hoffa disappear?

408 What *Dynasty* star sang off-key with the Hondells in the 1965 epic *Beach Blanket Bingo*?

409 What did New Jersey resident Eugene Schneider cut in half with a chain saw in 1976 to fulfill the equal division of property required by his divorce?

410 Of jock itch and athlete's foot, which is *tinea cruris*?

411 What white-collar profession has the highest suicide rate?

412 Which of Sammy Davis's eyes is the glass one?

413 For what crime was Michelle Triola Marvin arrested soon after her palimony suit settlement against Lee Marvin?

414 G. Gordon Liddy cooked and ate a rat to overcome fear of what?

415 In 1980, several employees of the Sunrise Hospital in Las Vegas were suspended for their unorthodox betting practices. What were they betting on?

416 With what leading man did Vivien Leigh hate performing love scenes because of his bad breath?

417 In William Golding's novel, what animal's head impaled on a stick was given the title "Lord of the Flies"?

418 What did Joan Crawford insist her children address her as?

419 Name one of the two people whom readers of *People* magazine voted, in a 1985 poll, they would least like to have lunch with.

420 What was Ernie Kovacs trying to do when he lost control of his car, causing its crash and his death?

421 What disease causes people to suddenly and unexpectedly fall asleep?

422 Giuseppe de Mai, a nineteenth-century Italian, had what extra organ in his body?

423 On average, what month sees the greatest number of homicides in New York City?

424 What actor described himself as having the eyes of a dead pig?

425 What was the name of the man identified by magazine ads as the developer and inventor of the famous bust-enlarging method?

426 What singer named his children Moon Unit and Dweezil?

427 During the 1968 presidential election campaign, who referred to Polish-Americans as "Polacks"?

428 What country was the first to declare war in World War I?

429 What TV evangelist claimed in October 1980 that God doesn't hear the prayers of Jews?

430 What rock and roll band had albums entitled *Goat's Head Soup* and *Sucking in the Seventies?*

431 What is the Black Death of the Middle Ages also known as?

432 In what 1970 film did Tom Selleck and Farrah Fawcett both appear?

Answers

1. Detroit
2. Idi Amin
3. The toilet seats
4. Gonorrhea
5. Benito Mussolini
6. Hanging and shooting
7. Their stomachs
8. Urine
9. Janis Joplin
10. Joan Collins
11. Ozzy Osbourne
12. W. C. Fields
13. The toothpick
14. Lee Trevino, Jerry Heard, Bobby Nichols
15. Evelyn
16. *Howdy Doody*
17. Dwight Eisenhower
18. Pennsylvania
19. The Damned
20. Mother-in-law killer
21. Caesar
22. Don Rickles
23. France
24. A pair of aces and a pair of eights
25. A cross-eyed woman
26. Abraham Zapruder
27. The common cold
28. *Lace*
29. The kidnap-murder of the Lindbergh baby
30. Tell all
31. People with skin diseases
32. Groucho Marx
33. Have sex
34. Jimi Hendrix
35. Dilaudin
36. Two
37. Two, Anne Boleyn and Catherine Howard
38. *Fanny Hill*
39. Karl Marx
40. Monday
41. Bela Lugosi
42. Her amputated leg
43. Wilbur Mills
44. Cocaine
45. A bird
46. Jacqueline Susann
47. A leg
48. Mick Jagger
49. Ivan the Terrible
50. Los Angeles International
51. *Pink Flamingos*
52. Monaco's Princess Caroline
53. An enema
54. Wendy Yoshimura
55. They burned them alive
56. Madonna
57. The cat
58. Shoes (10AAA)
59. A mixture of alcohol and drugs
60. Iowa
61. The western Pacific
62. Pussy
63. Barbara Bush
64. Spitting
65. Sonny and Cher
66. A turtle
67. Jehovah's Witness
68. Chocolate
69. Poodle
70. Errol Flynn
71. Dwight Eisenhower
72. Japan
73. Frank Rizzo, Philadelphia
74. The pig
75. He dropped dead
76. The Grand Wizard
77. Alice Cooper
78. Electrocution
79. Princess Margaret
80. Robert Mitchum
81. *Playboy*
82. Radiation poisoning
83. Because he spilled his seed upon the ground
84. Jim Palmer
85. Snake

86 Mae West
87 No mind
88 Sammy Davis, Jr.
89 The Mike Curb Congregation
90 Nevada
91 Urinating
92 A burglar
93 Van Halen
94 Edith Bunker
95 60–100
96 Babe Ruth
97 Their buttocks
98 Marlene Dietrich
99 Death
100 Thirty
101 Richard Nixon
102 Los Angeles
103 Eighty-one
104 Anissa Jones
105 Chuck Berry
106 Los Angeles Dodgers
107 Josef Stalin
108 Sid Vicious
109 A capon
110 Through the eardrum into the brain
111 For income tax evasion
112 Harvard
113 He dies
114 Adolf Hitler
115 The latrine
116 Barbara Stanwyck
117 Spider Sabich
118 Boston
119 H. Rap Brown

120 Australia
121 Firearms and explosives
122 German shepherd
123 da Vinci
124 Bill Murray
125 Utah
126 Zsa Zsa Gabor
127 A whale
128 Staten Island, New York
129 Fat Man
130 *Abbey Road*
131 A nymphomaniac
132 Jezebel (8th century B.C.)
133 In a pumpkin shell
134 The Divine Light Mission
135 *Santa Claus Conquers the Martians*
136 By a firing squad
137 1959
138 They were hanged
139 Clark Gable
140 A cactus
141 The penis
142 *The Tonight Show*
143 Gloria Steinem
144 Lung cancer
145 Asia
146 Twenty-eight
147 Alabama
148 His first wife Josephine's
149 Ivory Snow
150 The flush toilet
151 Ernest Hemingway
152 His clothes
153 That he was a homosexual

154 Washington, D.C.
155 Richard Nixon
156 Sacrificed himself, usually by fire
157 They were all males
158 *Midnight Cowboy*
159 He was Pope Alexander VI
160 Fingers or toes
161 Hemorrhoids
162 Andrew Jackson and Teddy Roosevelt
163 A Saint Bernard
164 MacKenzie Phillips
165 Charles Manson
166 *Our American Cousin*
167 They're too tight to sit down in
168 Robert Wagner and Christopher Walken
169 Its tongue
170 Complications from a perforated ulcer
171 Finland
172 Johnny Cash
173 Cutting/stabbing
174 Cleopatra
175 Mononucleosis
176 Lillian Carter
177 Sing Sing
178 Poodle
179 The National Cow Chip–Throwing Contest
180 She leapt from a six-story window
181 Human flesh
182 Cocaine
183 Abraham Lincoln

184 Michael Landon
185 Aristotle Onassis
186 Her pubic hair
187 In bed together
188 Mexico
189 Caryl Chessman
190 The Dead Kennedys
191 Victoria Principal
192 George Wallace
193 The left one
194 Ronald Reagan
195 Guyana
196 Alaska
197 Pussy Galore
198 Four
199 Groucho Marx
200 Over her bed
201 Egypt
202 Grace Slick
203 The Asian flu
204 Dave Garroway
205 Marlboro
206 Thirteen
207 Bird nests held together by bird mucus
208 Opium (and alcohol)
209 He was cheating on her
210 John Kennedy
211 Lewis Carroll
212 The left one
213 Red
214 *The Italian Stallion*
215 *Hair*

216 Judy Collins
217 Hanging
218 Ray Charles
219 Boston
220 Its gender
221 Moses
222 Tallulah Bankhead
223 Amputation of a leg
224 London's Heathrow Airport
225 Breasts
226 Ohio
227 Dennis Wilson
228 John Kennedy
229 A sheep
230 Richard Nixon
231 High blood pressure
232 William Henry Harrison
233 Chuck Barris
234 His corpse
235 Alabama
236 1972
237 Howard Hughes
238 Werner Erhard
239 Lake Tahoe
240 Jaclyn Smith
241 Ronald Reagan (Feb. '54)
242 Private Eddie Slovik
243 Leno and Rosemary LaBianca
244 1936
245 Little Johnny Green
246 Jerry Lewis
247 A hat
248 Posed nude in a magazine

249 Suicide (as of 1982)
250 Roy Rogers
251 Jim Morrison
252 Suicide
253 Jane Fonda
254 India
255 Sam Donaldson
256 William Howard Taft (over 300 lbs.)
257 Asthma
258 Hawaii
259 His brain
260 Playboy bunny
261 A mutt
262 On the sleeve or skirt
263 A breast
264 When it has never won a race
265 Rosie Ruiz
266 Elizabeth Taylor
267 Harry Truman
268 The mouse
269 Brian Wilson
270 Their beards
271 To try to buy her services for one night
272 Mao Tse-tung
273 Their manager, Brian Epstein
274 The West
275 Under the bed
276 Liberace
277 Taxes
278 Red, white, and blue
279 Renee Richards
280 His penis

281 David Soul
282 Friday
283 Koo Stark
284 Gypsy Rose Lee
285 The ear
286 The Panama Canal
287 Franklin Roosevelt
288 A U.S. flag
289 The following months
290 Poland
291 Humble pie
292 San Francisco
293 She had padded her bathing suit
294 Cher
295 *The Blob*
296 The sun
297 Austin
298 Marilyn Monroe
299 To be filmed
300 David Berkowitz
301 His illegitimate children by Tarita, Sr.
302 Four
303 Cass Elliot
304 In the gas chamber
305 Fat adults
306 Enrico Caruso
307 Linda Lovelace
308 Franklin Roosevelt
309 Her vagina
310 Winter
311 Angie Dickinson
312 13–14

313 Catherine the Great of Russia
314 The urine
315 Every twenty minutes
316 Buzz Aldrin
317 No one
318 Mark Twain
319 Andrew John
320 Their beards
321 A Cadillac
322 Hubert Humphrey
323 Eating
324 That they be killed
325 The blood of a sacrificial lamb
326 *The Catcher in the Rye*
327 Northern states
328 *Screw*
329 Al Green
330 The Vatican Library
331 $10,000
332 Witchcraft
333 A loose woman
334 Rudolph Valentino
335 The right side
336 Simon LeBon of Duran Duran
337 Eating
338 Billy Carter
339 The accordion
340 Liver disorders
341 William Holden
342 Martin Luther
343 He shot himself
344 George Wallace
345 He quit smoking

346 The bathroom
347 W. C. Fields
348 Ivory
349 A carrot
350 Coors
351 About 6000
352 Richard Pryor
353 Rod Stewart
354 She killed herself
355 444
356 She was raped
357 The turkey
358 An enema
359 Income tax evasion
360 U.S.C.
361 A toothache
362 A Pepsi commercial
363 Saturn
364 $5 million
365 Mondale-Ferraro
366 Spit into them
367 Janis Joplin
368 Cannibalism
369 The Lorraine Motel
370 Brazil
371 Jack Kerouac
372 Facial tissues
373 On tall poles around the house
374 The Boston Strangler
375 They're all dead
376 Suzette Charles
377 A heart attack
378 David Crosby

379 Ingmar Bergman
380 Twenty-eight days
381 The left one
382 Robert Blake
383 Tommy Rettig
384 Denmark
385 The chest
386 Marvin Gay, Sr.
387 Malaria
388 One of his ears
389 On his chin
390 Brian Jones
391 Hanging
392 Pornography
393 Groucho Marx
394 "Fire and Rain"
395 Sal Mineo
396 Mannequins
397 Thomas Jefferson

398 Roberto Rossellini
399 Michael Landon
400 Martin Luther
401 An armpit sniffer
402 Little Elvis
403 Thomas Edison
404 Her nose
405 Leukemia
406 The head of a Danish soldier
407 Detroit
408 Linda Evans
409 His $80,000 house
410 Jock itch
411 Pharmacists
412 The left one
413 Shoplifting
414 Rodents
415 How long certain patients would take to die

416 Clark Gable
417 A pig
418 Mommie Dearest
419 Nancy Reagan, Bernhard Goetz
420 Light his cigar with a wooden match
421 Narcolepsy
422 An extra heart
423 July
424 Marlon Brando
425 Mark Eden
426 Frank Zappa
427 Spiro Agnew
428 Austria-Hungary
429 Jerry Falwell
430 The Rolling Stones
431 The bubonic plague
432 *Myra Breckenridge*